BIG GREEN POETRY MACHINE

A World Of Wonder

Edited By Andrew Porter

First published in Great Britain in 2023 by:

Young Writers
Remus House
Coltsfoot Drive
Peterborough
PE2 9BF
Telephone: 01733 890066
Website: www.youngwriters.co.uk

All Rights Reserved
Book Design by Ashley Janson
© Copyright Contributors 2023
Softback ISBN 978-1-80459-524-4

Printed and bound in the UK by BookPrintingUK
Website: www.bookprintinguk.com
YB0541U

FOREWORD

Welcome Reader,

For Young Writers' latest competition The Big Green Poetry Machine, we asked primary school pupils to craft a poem about the world. From nature and environmental issues to exploring their own habitats or those of others around the globe, it provided pupils with the opportunity to share their thoughts and feelings about the world around them.

Here at Young Writers our aim is to encourage creativity in children and to inspire a love of the written word, so it's great to get such an amazing response, with some absolutely fantastic poems. It's important for children to be aware of the world around them and some of the issues we face, but also to celebrate what makes it great! This competition allowed them to express their hopes and fears or simply write about their favourite things. The Big Green Poetry Machine gave them the power of words and the result is a wonderful collection of inspirational and moving poems in a variety of poetic styles.

I'd like to congratulate all the young poets in this anthology; I hope this inspires them to continue with their creative writing.

CONTENTS

Craigour Park Primary School, Edinburgh

Milliejane McMillan (9)	1
Dalila Smail (9)	2
Rafeef Farah (9)	3
Olivia Fee (9)	4
Finlay Paterson (9)	5
Alexandra Costache (10)	6
Nicholas Krzewinski (9)	7
Leon Brown (9)	8
Ethan Dahlstrom (9)	9
Kristina MacRury (9)	10
Sharifa Haque (9)	11
Abigail Akpan Adigbob (9)	12
Albara El Fergani (9)	13
Alex Szulfer (9)	14
Elizabeth Sztuka (9)	15
Sarah Bouchouat (9)	16
Blaik Sharp (9)	17
Danny Chaney (9)	18
Evelyn McKeen (9)	19
Fergus McKeen (9)	20
Ksawery Sypien (10)	21
Maja Kryczyk (9)	22
Czarek Kocubowski (9)	23
David Sumilang (9)	24

Meon Junior School, Southsea

Kate Liddicott (9)	25
Florence Marques Cann (10)	26
Iris Canning (7)	28
Oscar Boulton (8)	30
Felicity Houghton (9)	31
Evie Ayres (9)	32

Ellie Day (10)	33
Callie Radcliffe (7)	34
Joseph Rogers (9)	35
Abbygail Lu (9)	36
Yash Yaram (8)	37
Emmanuella Olaoluwa (10)	38
Monica Boscaro (10)	39
Alena-Grace Basiyalo (8)	40
Harry Worley (7)	41
Ananya Patel (7)	42
Nikos Zardavas Serrano (8)	43
Niya Tsankaora (8)	44
Olivia Weetch (8)	45

North Bridge House Pre-Prep School, London

Lucio Ruggeri (6)	46
David Ellis (6)	47
DanDan Bershadsky (6)	48
Jing Cheng Chong (6)	50
Viyan Bragadees (7)	51
Keito Akazawa (7)	52
Sasha Nelson (7)	53
Sham Sweid (6)	54
Tiril Støve (7)	55
Hayley Chung (7)	56
Zach Glozer (7)	57
Hannah Belchier (5)	58
Luca Formisano-Barata (6)	59
Raania Rahman (6)	60
Ishaan Singh (6)	61
Andrey Gurski (6)	62
Benjamin Saffon (6)	63
Pietro Pane De Bartolomeis (6)	64
Matt Bonin (7)	65

Name	No.
Tsubaki Fukazawa (6)	66
Takahiro Matsumoto (5)	67
Charlie Norman (7)	68
Rey Park (5)	69
Rye Harbour (6)	70
Evie Dennis (5)	71
Leah Atkin (7)	72
Leo Cassen (6)	73
Clara Driver (5)	74
Sybil Barrett-Haigh (5)	75
Maya Bloch (6)	76
Leo Shuck (7)	77
Kian Kapoor (6)	78
Nestor Knysh (6)	79
Aayan Gowribalan-Khan (5)	80
Michael Masterson (6)	81
Xavier Mistry (6)	82
Daren Yi (6)	83
Kailhan Varatharajan (5)	84
Anaïs Strauss (6)	85
Layla Zaghloul (6)	86
Issy Armstrong (5)	87
Rocco Recksik (6)	88
Matteo Naghib (7)	89
Sashi Dimitrov (5)	90
Georgina Taub (5)	91
Xander Sijuwade (5)	92
Timur Lim (6)	93
Thomas Gatt (7)	94
Jack Lees (7)	95
Amro Elatfy (6)	96
Gabriel Chazot (7)	97
Sofia Smodis (6)	98
Fedor Kirichun (7)	99
Leon Caville (6)	100

Our Lady Queen Of Peace Catholic Engineering College, Skelmersdale

Name	No.
Harvey Lewis Thomas Lloyd (12)	101
Evie Scrafton (12)	102
Kayden Lewin (11)	104
Kelsie Cook (11)	105
Lucas Ratcliffe (12)	106
Peyton Kelly (11)	108
McKenzie-Leigh Gregson (12)	109
Macey-Leigh Levy (11)	110
Lola McGann (12)	111
Olly McGovern (11)	112
Finley McLoughlin Cookson (11)	113
Raygn Lancaster-Lyness (12)	114
Jazmine Williams (11)	115
Hannah Moorcroft (11)	116
Ketija Pajate (11)	117
Scarlett Macgregor (12)	118
Kristers Kalnins (11)	119
Emilija Pajate (12)	120
Enzo Johnson (11)	121
Ethan Byrne (12)	122
Tyler James (11)	123
Matthew Hislop (12)	124
Maisie Ridgway (11)	125
Rebeca Palma (11)	126
Juliana Varga (12)	127
Jorja Jones (11)	128
Hope Sorrell (11)	129
Kaci Williams (12)	130
Alex Rowles (12)	131
Oskar Slojewski (11)	132
Poppy Causer (12)	133
Summer Levy (11)	134
Damien Rakoncsa (12)	135
Carmel Pierce (12)	136
Ellis Houghton (11)	137
Kenzi O'Donnell (11)	138
Lacey Ledden (11)	139
Isobel Farley (12)	140
Maddie Abbott (11)	141
Xavier Naumovicz (11)	142
Miley Rae Davies (12)	143
Abiah Kamran (11)	144
Jacek Kwapisiewicz (12)	145
Leon Janowski (11)	146
Lee Ives (11)	147
Evie Hutton (11)	148
Teegan Graves (12)	149

Amelia O'Brien Roberts (11)	150
Ayden Denton (11)	151
Daniel Spencer (11)	152
Jake Chatterley (12)	153
Savannah Corrie (12)	154
Harley Goodier-Davies (11)	155
Ava Smith (11)	156
Zach Dickson (11)	157
Isaac Moore (12)	158
Bethany Brown (12)	159
James McCormick (12)	160
Scott Pittman (12)	161
Nathan Figura (11)	162

St Paul's Catholic Primary School, Cheshunt

Graciella Kusi-Appiah (9)	163
Ela Capar (9)	164
Yvette Van Molendorff (10)	166
Oscar Overett (8)	168
Hannah Powell (10)	169
Alessadro Moreno Mendez (10)	170
James Kelly (8)	171
Olivia Kelly (10)	172
Lucas Layton (10)	173
Scarlett Curtin-McKen (9)	174
Poppy Ward (8)	175
Daniel O'Neill (9)	176
Grace O'Sullivan (10)	177
Savina D'Oca (7)	178
Kieron Lusanta (11)	179
Kara Hodson (10)	180
Liberty Connolly (8)	181
Bianca Avram (9)	182
Alexie Chitolie (9)	183
Elisabeta Neculai (9)	184
Aoife Esther Keady (10)	185
Olivier Kaszuba (8)	186
Blake Smith (10)	187
Maya Allen (9)	188
Ellie-May Goldhawk (8)	189
Jasper Palmer (10)	190
Lorena Aliberti (10)	191

Giovanni Arango Kasa (9)	192
Fearne Popely (8)	193
Adriano Nicolaou (10)	194
Dexter Breaks	195
Fiana Miltiadou (8)	196
Tommy Parry (8)	197
Jude Smith (8)	198
Louie Costello (9)	199
Rees Ohene (11)	200
Luca Amodei (10)	201
George Amdrose (9)	202
Reggie-James Miles (9)	203
Jacob Robins (9)	204
Christian Manaois (7)	205
Alessia Caruso (8)	206
Ruby Doherty (10)	207
Meghna Boojhowon (8)	208
Kameron Prodromou (9)	209
Maya Rosinska (8)	210
Kayla Okeke (10)	211
Sidelya Kalen (8)	212
Gabriel Hristov (8)	213
John O'Sullivan (7)	214
Matteo Amodei (7)	215
Carolina Platon (9)	216
Kaiya Prodromou (8)	217
River Cullen (11)	218
Aiden Hussein (9)	219
Faolan Saunders (11)	220
Andy Cash (11)	221
Ezekiel Baker (10)	222
Malakai Amali Rowland (10)	223
Aurora D'Alessandro (10)	224
Taylor Anthony-Alphonse (7)	225
Ella-Louise Whitmore (10)	226
Mason Valladares (7)	227
Gabriel Hristov (8)	228
Joseph Vieira Palushaj (8)	229
Hayden Paton (8)	230

THE POEMS

Polar Bears

P ollution is hurting our animals
O ver in the Arctic, polar bears need help.
L ife is hard and they are nearly extinct because it is
A dangerous time with the icebergs melting, so please
R ecycle your rubbish.

B e kind to the environment, our
E arth is dying.
A ll I see are polar bears being separated
R ight now. Think of the polar bears.
S ave the polar bears.

Milliejane McMillan (9)
Craigour Park Primary School, Edinburgh

Recycle

- **R** euse and recycle.
- **E** arth is dirty and full of plastic.
- **C** arry your recycling and put it in an empty bin.
- **Y** our little bit of rubbish that you might have thrown on the floor can cause a big problem.
- **C** hocolate wrappers and crisp bags are all over the ground.
- **L** ive animals like gulls are eating the rubbish or getting stuck in plastic bags.
- **E** veryone has a responsibility to take care of the planet.

Dalila Smail (9)
Craigour Park Primary School, Edinburgh

Animals

A lot of animals are going extinct.
N ot all get fed and people are starving.
I don't even know why this is happening anymore.
M ore because they are killing way too many.
A nimals are dying because of food as well.
L ots of animals are going extinct because people are hungry.
S ea animals are dying, more animals and people are still starving.

Rafeef Farah (9)
Craigour Park Primary School, Edinburgh

Our Planet

O ur planet is dying
U se your heart and respect our planet
R espect the animals, seas, and oceans.

P eople live on this planet as well
L ives are in danger
A t times there are wildfires and animals lose their homes
N ot all animals have homes when born
E co-friendly is a thing and let's make our planet
T hat!

Olivia Fee (9)
Craigour Park Primary School, Edinburgh

What Am I?

I am big and blue and you live on me.
There are over thirty countries on me.
I am round like a basketball.
I am one of the eight planets in the solar system.
Animals are dying on me and becoming extinct.
Animals live on me too and they are really cool.
Over eight billion people live on me.
There are many houses on me.
What am I?

Answer: *The Earth*.

Finlay Paterson (9)
Craigour Park Primary School, Edinburgh

Rewild

R emember our animals are losing their homes.
E very day trash affects our creatures! The
W ild is not in the best shape for them!
  I f the animals are saying, "Help us," we will try our best to help.
L ove them, don't kill. If the bees die, no more nature!
D ead or not dead, they will still be in our hearts.

Alexandra Costache (10)
Craigour Park Primary School, Edinburgh

Pollution

P lastic in the oceans is really bad.
O ceans are in a bad state.
L et's save the world.
L ook at the ocean, it's so dirty. Let's fix this.
U s. We will help clean the oceans.
T he ocean is really
I mportant.
O ur world is changing.
N ever throw plastic in the ocean.

Nicholas Krzewinski (9)
Craigour Park Primary School, Edinburgh

Our Planet

O ur rainforests are getting sick
U se help from the city
R ecycling is good for the Earth.

P ollution is bad for the world
L and is not happy
A nd we need to do something about that
N o more littering for the world
E nvironment is in danger
T aking land from the world.

Leon Brown (9)
Craigour Park Primary School, Edinburgh

What Am I?

I live on the frozen waters of Antarctica.
I am slowly becoming endangered.
I eat a lot of fish.
I like to swim.
I have not got many places to live.
People have polluted my lands.
What was white is now green.
I have been deported to far-away zoos.

Answer: A penguin.

Ethan Dahlstrom (9)
Craigour Park Primary School, Edinburgh

What Am I?

What am I?

I am blue, fast and flowing.
I can be deep.
I can be shallow.
I am cold and I am hot depending on the weather.
Many beings live inside me.
Sometimes I am dangerous.
Other times I am calm.

What am I?

Answer: *The ocean.*

Kristina MacRury (9)
Craigour Park Primary School, Edinburgh

Save The Rhinos

R hinos have lives just like us.
H elp the rhinos.
I f people don't stop killing rhinos then there will be no more rhinos.
N ow the rhinos are endangered.
O nce the rhinos were safe and happy, now they are scared for their lives.

Sharifa Haque (9)
Craigour Park Primary School, Edinburgh

11

What Am I?

I am round.
I am sometimes warm and sometimes cold.
I have one moon.
I am being polluted by people.
I am one of eight of my kind.
I am the third closest to the sun.
Stop polluting the environment.
What am I?

Answer: *The Earth.*

Abigail Akpan Adigbob (9)
Craigour Park Primary School, Edinburgh

Polar Bears

Polar bears live in the North Pole
Over and under, ice is melting
All the polar bears are becoming extinct
Life in the North Pole is disappearing
But there is still hope
Even a bit of help will save them
A life with no joy
Rewild us and save us.

Albara El Fergani (9)
Craigour Park Primary School, Edinburgh

Save The Earth

I am not happy
I am sad
I am dying
I am extinct
I need help
I need protecting
I have animals needing help
I have plastic in my oceans.

You can recycle
You can plant trees
You can keep the animals safe
Save the Earth.

Alex Szulfer (9)
Craigour Park Primary School, Edinburgh

Orangutans

I have no name.
I live on the ground which is making my species die.
I used to roam the trees and have the tropical sun on my back,
But now only babies of my species are protected.
Now I see sand where my home is supposed to be.

Elizabeth Sztuka (9)
Craigour Park Primary School, Edinburgh

Ocean

O ver the seas.
C ould that be litter flying around the ocean?
E verybody keeps doing this. It needs to stop!
A ny time fish can die from it.
N ever throw plastic in the ocean.

Sarah Bouchouat (9)
Craigour Park Primary School, Edinburgh

What Am I?

I am green and blue.
I am in a universe.
You live on me
I have some mountains.
I have rivers.
My inhabitants drop litter on me.
What am I?

Answer: Earth.

Blaik Sharp (9)
Craigour Park Primary School, Edinburgh

Earth

E verything is dying at once
A nd we should step in
R ight now and stop this because
T ogether we can help the environment
H elp. Not kill.

Danny Chaney (9)
Craigour Park Primary School, Edinburgh

The Big Green Poetry Machine - A World Of Wonder

What Am I?

I'm endangered
I'm losing my habitat
My kind are dying
I'm heavily guarded
I'm rough and tough
What am I?

Answer: A rhino.

Evelyn McKeen (9)
Craigour Park Primary School, Edinburgh

What Am I?

I am in danger
I am burning with fire
I am getting cut down
I am disappearing due to climate change.
What am I?

Answer: Trees.

Fergus McKeen (9)
Craigour Park Primary School, Edinburgh

My Planet

Earth is a nice planet
People should stop throwing plastic
This is bad for the Earth
It is killing animals
I want to live on a peaceful planet.

Ksawery Sypien (10)
Craigour Park Primary School, Edinburgh

Weather

The weather was beautiful.
The weather was stormy.
The weather was rainy.
The weather was sunny.
The weather is changing all the time.

Maja Kryczyk (9)
Craigour Park Primary School, Edinburgh

Save The World

Do not drop litter in the city
Save the world and animals
People are dying
Others are ill in hospitals
Take care of our world.

Czarek Kocubowski (9)
Craigour Park Primary School, Edinburgh

Climate Change
A kennings poem

Ice melting
Wildfires starting
Cities flooding
Polar bears dying
Rhinos thirsty
Weather crazy
Trees falling.

David Sumilang (9)
Craigour Park Primary School, Edinburgh

The Forest

Every day the forest starts to grow
The goodness in the world seems to glow
But every time a tree is chopped
That goodness is then dropped
For every seed that's planted
Ten lumber mills have started
For every breath we take
A factory chain starts like a snake
For every good thing done
All the bad things make it feel like none
In the darkness it seems like we're done
But light has shone
Giving us light from beyond
For there is hope for every little frond
We are starting to realise what we've done
And that it can't be covered with a bad pun
We are saving Earth now, not later
We have to think of everyone, even alligators
And now that trees are growing
That goodness is once again glowing.

Kate Liddicott (9)
Meon Junior School, Southsea

The Best Season Of Them All

Every year, good or bad,
The seasons pass and go!
From spring to summer to autumn to winter.
Let's find out a bit more about them.

First, we have spring:
Mother of months March, April and May,
Also having the celebration of Easter,
Children are messing about for April Fools,
As blossoms of beauty shelter them from the blinding sun.

Next up we've got summer:
An energetic season to say the least,
Caretaker of June, July and August,
Funky with fourth of July's blasting fireworks,
But also relaxing with the rays of the sun from the summer solstice.

Here comes autumn and a strong breeze,
Parent of September, October and November,

Ready to give you a fright with the spirit of Halloween,
Rain pouring from the grey clouds above.

Last but not the least, winter,
Giving a chill down your spine,
But don't worry or be scared,
As the merry joy of Christmas will warm your heart,
As the family gets together,
Snowmen are being made as well as joyous memories.

So, no matter what!
Every season and every year will be a fun twist.
But now it's up to you to decide:
What's your favourite season?

Florence Marques Cann (10)
Meon Junior School, Southsea

Tree Lily's Life

I am a tree,
There are over 60,000 species of me.
I have lots of branches to spread my leaves out,
So that they can absorb the sun, keeping me healthy, no doubt.

I grow near anything I see,
Lots of children like climbing up me.
I've been alive for thousands of years,
During this time I've shed lots of tears.

People are trying to kill me,
They won't just stop and let me be.
Don't they know I help them breathe?
Creating oxygen to help them believe.

Believe that it's okay to ruin the planet,
By dropping rubbish, that can't be right, can it?
Please take your rubbish home, or even better, recycle it,
Look after the world, you'll only get one of it.

I am a tree, as cute as can be,
Helping the world be a nice place to be.
So don't drop litter on the floor or dirty the sea,
Keep the world clean. From the planet, and me.

Iris Canning (7)
Meon Junior School, Southsea

Pollution And A Sea Turtle

I am a turtle, I spend my time in the ocean,
My outer shell's strong, my eyesight not so much,
So when it comes to eating food, I really must take care,
For not everything I come across is as it seems,
I sometimes snack on jellyfish, not everybody knows,
I often mistake them for plastic bags which end up in my nose,
I don't have hands or any tools to help me get them out,
I drift, I wait, there's nothing I can do,
If only I could talk, I would tell you this isn't nice,
I deserve to eat my meal without a risk to life,
Each day I live in fear, not knowing which way to turn,
The ocean could be so beautiful if we only listened and learned.

Oscar Boulton (8)
Meon Junior School, Southsea

A Changing World

A postcard came for me today.
A picture-perfect postcard of a beautiful island.
With golden sands, crystal clear, blue water and green, green palm trees.
I saw fish all brightly coloured, swimming happily in the sea.
And a crab on the glistening sand, bathing in the sun.
It looked like paradise and I longed to be there.

I looked out of my window today, a view that was grey and dull.
With high raised buildings, murky water and grey smoke that filled the air.
I saw layers of plastic bobbing in the sea, and lines of cars, exhaust fumes flowing behind.
This is not paradise but pollution, and where I call home.

Felicity Houghton (9)
Meon Junior School, Southsea

Eco-Savers

Save the environment,
It is too precious to destroy.
Save the ecosystem,
Stop letting factories employ,
For they are releasing gases that are not good for the air,
And people cutting down trees, well, they just do not care.
If these people carry on,
Where will all those animals belong?
To conclude, I must say to you,
Before you go, a thing or two,
Like before you go to jump in your car,
Ask yourself, "Are we really going that far?"
If you're not, I would like
For you to ride, instead, your bike.
If you see an eco-hater,
Say, "Stop, I'm an eco-saver!"

Evie Ayres (9)
Meon Junior School, Southsea

Save Our World

The Earth is dark and grey
Because the pollution is getting in the way
Let's do our bit and recycle bottles, tins, paper and plastic
Put it in the bin provided for you!
Do you really want these animals to suffer all because of us?
We should act tougher and stop causing a fuss
Help our creatures big and small
By planting trees that grow tall
It will help our planet to be greener
To make our planet cleaner
Get on your bike and cycle
It helps you get fit and it's vital
Put your cars away
And use foot power to be healthy, hooray!

Ellie Day (10)
Meon Junior School, Southsea

The Journey Of Rubbish

Hey, just think about where your rubbish ends up every day
Don't worry, it's just started
When you go to the beach
Each little piece swishes into the sea
It can travel a long, long way, you know
To Africa, to America, to Antarctica, even to Portsmouth
Also, things can sink
A plastic bag can look like a jellyfish
And to marine life can look like a delicious dish
Bottles can drift and drift
A terrific tiger might think it's a sparkling fish
So put your rubbish in the bin.

Callie Radcliffe (7)
Meon Junior School, Southsea

The Solution

There is a lot of pollution,
What is the solution?
There are lots of fumes that come from your car,
If you make a journey, don't make it far!
Burning coal, oil and gas is going to spoil our atmosphere.
Let's burn less and keep the air clear.
A big, beautiful sea,
It should be plastic-free.
We can get our power from a wind farm,
It will do the planet less harm.
So, what's the solution? What should we do?
I think the solution is me and you!

Joseph Rogers (9)
Meon Junior School, Southsea

Save The Environment

Save the Earth,
Protect the planet,
Don't forget to recycle plastic.
Help the rainforest and also creatures,
But watch out! There are leeches.
Don't worry if you can't finish it all,
It would be helpful though if you were very tall.
Mums, dads and teachers are all helping,
So don't worry, you'll get through this.
Save pollution. Oh, bliss!
But if we work as a team,
You'll get to your biggest dream.

Abbygail Lu (9)
Meon Junior School, Southsea

Plants And Trees

Plants and trees
Sway with the breeze,
Dancing left to right,
Oh tree, you're so lush,
And when your leaves fall slowly,
They turn into mush,
You give me and everyone air,
That's very fair,
Sadly there's global warming,
Forest fires are rapidly swarming,
Yes, this is alarming,
People are chopping trees
For their greedy needs,
To factories they send,
Is this really the end?

Yash Yaram (8)
Meon Junior School, Southsea

Reduce, Reuse, Recycle

Let's recycle, there is so much plastic.
Let's recycle, it's fantastic.
Don't forget about paper and glasses.
Recycle together.

When you see litter in the streets,
And the air smells of pollution,
When you feel like it's piling up,
Remember, there is a solution.
Don't be a punk, recycle your junk.
Don't litter, it makes the world bitter.

Emmanuella Olaoluwa (10)
Meon Junior School, Southsea

The Mole Who Would

I can't be heard under the earth
I can't be seen amongst the green
Please help, my home is being destroyed
All the beautiful trees disappearing without a trace
Oh, please help me save this special place
Just little things like turning off a tap
Or switching off a light switch with a zap
Anything please, just to do good
For I am only a mole who would if I could!

Monica Boscaro (10)
Meon Junior School, Southsea

Solution For Pollution

Do not throw your rubbish in the ocean,
It can cause quite a commotion,
For all the sea creatures that call it home,
They will suffer as they roam,
Dirty, unsafe water will make animals sickly,
With toxic waste spreading diseases quickly
So, as a nation,
We can do better for the next generation,
To find a solution,
For all this pollution.

Alena-Grace Basiyalo (8)
Meon Junior School, Southsea

Climate Change

Why are your ice caps getting so low,
On your famous, beautiful snow?
But in other countries, is it so hot?
But in your country, it is not?
And why are polar bears getting so warm?
Look at them, fanning themselves at dawn!
Did we not learn the lessons of the Lorax?
Take climate change seriously and take in the facts!

Harry Worley (7)
Meon Junior School, Southsea

Happy Sunny Day!

Once it was a sunny day and the sun was really bright
The sun was always happy because the world was beautiful
The children were playing outside and the plants were growing
Some farmers were really happy because their vegetables were growing
Then everyone came into the garden and shouted, "Happy sunny day!"

Ananya Patel (7)
Meon Junior School, Southsea

My Three Haikus Of Nature

Plastic is super
Recycle and don't make more
To care for nature.

The pollution is
Bad for the environment
The Earth needs some help.

Rubbish and plastic
Our world full of plastic does
Not biodegrade.

Nikos Zardavas Serrano (8)
Meon Junior School, Southsea

Let's Save Trees!

Drawing is nice
But we're killing trees!
Without trees we have no oxygen
Without trees animals and people can't live
So let's try not to kill trees
And start drawing on the front and back of paper.

Niya Tsankaora (8)
Meon Junior School, Southsea

Recycle Bin

It's not fantastic to use plastic,
It's important to recycle,
Skip the car, use a bicycle,
Plastic bottles, metal tins,
Do not belong in your bins,
Do not be a din,
Put it in your recycle bin.

Olivia Weetch (8)
Meon Junior School, Southsea

Snail In The Garden

S imon the snail, slithering along
N ow he meets his friends
A long the way in the luscious garden
I nsects, birds and bees, what a sight to see!
L uckily for Simon, he has a shell to protect himself.

I nside the shell, Simon feels cosy
N ice and warm, ready to eat the fuzzy plants.

T he time has come for him to wake
H appy slithering, munching the plants
E arly in the morning, Simon sleeps.

G athering at dawn, the birds, bees and butterflies
A re all together, happy in the rain
R eady to play an important part in helping
D eliver a healthy ecosystem
E very insect and bird is precious
N ature is everything, protect it, don't hurt it!

Lucio Ruggeri (6)
North Bridge House Pre-Prep School, London

Protect The Forest

It's so nice to have a forest
Where there are trees and birds and squirrels
Look at that bird, so cosy in its nest
But if there was no forest, everyone would die
The birds would be cold without a home
The squirrels would be hungry without any pine nuts
And the oxygen from the trees that we need for breathing would not be there anymore.

So now you have learned your lesson
Of what the world would be like without the trees in the forest
You know it's not a joke!
We must look after the environment, it's the truth!

We must protect the planet!
The trees, the water and the animals
Make sure you don't chop the trees in the forest
Or leave rubbish that can make the animals die
And the forest will stay nice.

David Ellis (6)
North Bridge House Pre-Prep School, London

Hampstead Heath Park

When I go to the park
I see swans laying eggs
The grass swaying on my feet
Brown leaves falling
Flowers blooming
Light wind coming back and again
And dandelions turning into clocks.

During the day, I hear birds singing
And feel sunshine on my face
I see foxes coming out at night to eat
And I listen to the owl's hoot before finding their prey.

I smell the cold, fresh air
Feel the ants beneath my feet
See my face shining in the pond
And dogs leaping at balls
I see people playing tennis on the courts
I hear walking people chattering
And kids on swings.

The park makes me happy
The park makes me feel good about myself.

DanDan Bershadsky (6)
North Bridge House Pre-Prep School, London

Our Planet

R ainforests are in danger, the green bits will disappear.
A big tree will be nothing, you know it's not fair.
I know you know we know, so don't mess with it.
N o, it's not fair if you just don't care.
F orests are not like this, they are the lungs of planet Earth.
O r if there are no rainforests, there will only be eighty percent of the air.
R esting is boring, explore the scenery of the rainforest.
E ven if you are bored with your garden, it will be good to see a rainforest.
S o get out there where you can explore this planet.
T he rainforests are green and bugs and animals will be there.

Jing Cheng Chong (6)
North Bridge House Pre-Prep School, London

The Wonders Of Rain

Rain helps animals drink
If animals didn't have anything to drink
They could actually die
Plants also drink rain
But sometimes when it's raining really heavily
You should stay inside and keep warm and safe
If there is a lot of rain
If you have a garden and you planted many seeds
Or one seed
You could look out of the window
And you could see that your seed has grown
Into a big plant
And you could plant a vegetable seed
And when it rains it will grow into a beautiful plant
Rain is important for worms
Because earthworms like living in damp places
Like the forest
And animals need rain.

Viyan Bragadees (7)
North Bridge House Pre-Prep School, London

Our Planet

P enguins pop out of the water,
E ating fish is what penguins do,
N ever can fly but swimming is what penguins do,
G ive up penguins? Please don't, because penguins are amazing,
U nique penguins stand out in Antarctica,
I hope penguins don't go extinct,
N o one can survive where they live unless they have special clothes made for the cold,
S ee them swimming majestically.

Keito Akazawa (7)
North Bridge House Pre-Prep School, London

Coral Reef

C alm above but chatter below
O rcas swim above, not caring about the life below
R ough, red coral below the surface
A lgae and seagrass cover everything in green
L ittle fish swim happily, chasing each other.

R ainbow coral welcomes the life around it
E cosystem under the water
E ndangered by humans
F ish lose their homes.

Look after our oceans!

Sasha Nelson (7)
North Bridge House Pre-Prep School, London

Our Planet

I am a tree, please don't cut me.
I give you oxygen, I am the lungs of Earth.
I am a tree, please don't cut me.
I provide you with yummy fruits and vegetables.
I am a tree, please don't cut me.
You can play under my shadow and climb on me.
I am a tree, please don't cut me.
I am the house of many creatures.
I am a tree, please don't cut me.
I am the green colour of Earth.

Sham Sweid (6)
North Bridge House Pre-Prep School, London

Polar Bears

P olar bears live in the Arctic.
O n the snow, they stomp everywhere
L ooking for homes to sleep.
A *re there friends out there?* he wonders.
R ocking on a melting ice flake.

B e the kindest to our planet.
E arth is getting warmer.
A ll of us need to be better.
R escue the animals!
S ave the polar bears!

Tiril Støve (7)
North Bridge House Pre-Prep School, London

Waterfalls

W aterfalls fall very quickly
A mazing levels I don't understand
T he water flies everywhere
E ven I get wet sometimes
R ight this way, I see one
F ollow leaves falling in the water
A t speeds I do need
L ovely, fun drops to slide off
L ean forwards and get ready to drown
S uch things mustn't be played with.

Hayley Chung (7)
North Bridge House Pre-Prep School, London

Waterfalls

W ater descending down the fall
A sparkly glimmer down the fall
T he big rocks on both sides
E ither right or left
R ewarding to look at
F ascinating to see
A ll of it is one big surprise
L ike or dislike, I hope you like
L ovely and cool and nice and splattery
S till, waterfalls fascinate me.

Zach Glozer (7)
North Bridge House Pre-Prep School, London

Forest School

F illing a pond
O utdoor fun
R ock collecting
E njoying fresh air
S eeing bird nests
T rees all around.

S mokey campfires
C heese sandwiches
H elp feed the birds
O ften in muddy puddles
O n the big, blue bus
L earning about nature.

Hannah Belchier (5)
North Bridge House Pre-Prep School, London

The Great Wind

Wind is cold
Wind is air
Wind is big and everywhere.

Wind is good for ships
Wind is good for the Earth
Wind is good for you
Wind has been here since the planet's birth.

Wind can be strong like a gust
Wind can be soft like a breeze
Wind can be big like a hurricane
Wind can hug and kiss the trees.

Luca Formisano-Barata (6)
North Bridge House Pre-Prep School, London

The Oak Tree

T he oak tree stands
H alfway between house and road
E very branch full of leaves.

O n one branch a swing
A squirrel sometimes comes
K een to eat the acorns.

T he crumbs are on the swing
R obins hop around the tree
E very Christmas
E very year.

Raania Rahman (6)
North Bridge House Pre-Prep School, London

Our Planet

O ne Earth that we have
U rgent to save it
R ising sea levels because of melting ice.

P ollution makes Earth hotter
L ittering pollutes Earth
A nimals are dying
N ow stop littering, everyone
E ach of us must be kinder to our planet
T ogether we can save Earth!

Ishaan Singh (6)
North Bridge House Pre-Prep School, London

Our Planet

G ardens are relaxing but always need tidying.
A utumn is when the crispy, crunchy leaves fall.
R ain makes the flowers grow.
D uring spring I dig the soft, brown soil to find treasure.
E very day I tidy the leaves and hear planes in the sky.
N ight-time is dark and Randy the cat goes to bed.

Andrey Gurski (6)
North Bridge House Pre-Prep School, London

Cheetahs

They're as fast as light.
Spots all around.
Fastest living cat.
Spots for camouflage.
Balance from their tail.
As fierce as a monster and cute little cubs.
How do their cubs look like honey badgers?
It's so interesting and wonderful.
They live in the savannahs.
They are my favourite animal.

Benjamin Saffon (6)
North Bridge House Pre-Prep School, London

My Dog

My dog is twelve.
He was strong
But now he is old.
When he was a puppy he liked to play,
But now he likes to sleep and eat.
When we go upstairs he cries
Because we are not there.
His name is Brando,
He lives in Italy in a small town.
He lives with my grandpa and grandma
In a small castle.

Pietro Pane De Bartolomeis (6)
North Bridge House Pre-Prep School, London

The Blue Planet

I can smell some stinky pollution.
I hate pollution.
I want to see some lovely blue sea.
The blue planet is in very bad danger!
There is too much pollution.
Don't turn our planet grey, turn it blue.
Don't destroy our lovely planet.
Make sure you keep our planet as blue as the sky!

Matt Bonin (7)
North Bridge House Pre-Prep School, London

The Earth

The Earth has to be clean
Because if the Earth is dirty
The Earth will be boiling hot
And maybe the Arctic
Animals live there
But if the ice cracks
And polar bears don't have much space
They might die!
And humans don't want that!
So we have to protect the animals.

Tsubaki Fukazawa (6)
North Bridge House Pre-Prep School, London

Our Planet: Spring

S eason of sunny days succeeding winter.
P icnic in the park is a pleasure, people can feel the season coming.
R ainy days are gone.
I n the garden, a range of plants start blossoming.
N o snow can be seen.
G round is full of flowers.

Takahiro Matsumoto (5)
North Bridge House Pre-Prep School, London

Axel Foley

  A mazing little dog
e **X** cited dog
  E njoys eating ham
  L ovely, slobbery tongue.

  F un
  O ver me he climbs in bed
  L oving little dog
  E njoys licking faces
  Y ou will love him when you see him.

Charlie Norman (7)
North Bridge House Pre-Prep School, London

Save Narwhals

N arwhals are very beautiful.
A re you going to see them in the future?
R eady to see them?
W ild animals are in danger.
H elp them live safely.
A ll we need to do is take care of them.
L ove and save narwhals!

Rey Park (5)
North Bridge House Pre-Prep School, London

Grotty Garbage

G rotty, sticky, smelly!
A ll around my garden
R ubbish thrown away all day
B ins with trash getting fuller
A nd fuller until they explode
G rotesque, messy, ghastly!
"E co warriors, save the plants!"

Rye Harbour (6)
North Bridge House Pre-Prep School, London

Our Planet

Trees grow very tall
When the wind blows they can fall
I love trees, they help me breathe
In the spring they grow their leaves
So many colours I can't believe!
They are good for climbing way up high
Until I can almost touch the birds in the sky.

Evie Dennis (5)
North Bridge House Pre-Prep School, London

Nature

Nature takes care of animals and beautiful plants.
Nature also has deadly plants like thorns and stinging nettles.
Mother Nature made this amazing world.
Please respect nature or else it will hit you with thorns or stinging nettles.
Don't hurt animals!

Leah Atkin (7)
North Bridge House Pre-Prep School, London

Summer

In summer flowers bloom on mountains,
And I run through water fountains.
In summer it's my birthday!
I blow balloons, but some fly away.
I can see three birds flying with glee,
Flapping about around me.
The happiness of summer.

Leo Cassen (6)
North Bridge House Pre-Prep School, London

Koalas

K oalas are in danger, we need to save the day!
O n trees they climb.
A s bushfires strike their homes.
L ots of danger is around, so help!
A s off they go through the trees.
S o many reasons to help!

Clara Driver (5)
North Bridge House Pre-Prep School, London

Traffic

T errible traffic in London
R ight on our doorsteps
A ffecting our lungs
F ocusing on reducing pollution
F or everyone's health
I t is important to drive less
C hange is possible.

Sybil Barrett-Haigh (5)
North Bridge House Pre-Prep School, London

Outside

I love being outside
Nature makes me happy
Birds flying around
Squirrels scuttling up trees
Running and jumping through the leaves
Smelling the fresh air
Wind in my hair
I love being outside
It's always so fun.

Maya Bloch (6)
North Bridge House Pre-Prep School, London

Winter And Autumn

I love winter because there is lots of white, soft snow
And the lights on the Christmas tree glow.
I like autumn because it's my birthday
And it's always a fun day.
These are the reasons
For my favourite seasons.

Leo Shuck (7)
North Bridge House Pre-Prep School, London

My Yellow Aeroplane

My yellow aeroplane flies so high,
Shining and glimmering in the blue sky.
My yellow aeroplane shoots bullets and bombs,
Keeping Ukraine safe and strong.
My yellow aeroplane is my favourite toy,
Making me a very happy boy!

Kian Kapoor (6)
North Bridge House Pre-Prep School, London

The Environment

F eel nature beside you
O r stick with friends and family and make campfires
R each the broken nests
E co things all around
S o I'd rather stick together
T he animals are very cute!

Nestor Knysh (6)
North Bridge House Pre-Prep School, London

Save Our Planet

The planet is beautiful,
You should think it is wonderful.
Our planet is blue and green,
It is important to keep it clean.
Everyone should pick up litter and recycle plastic,
Then the Earth would be super fantastic.

Aayan Gowribalan-Khan (5)
North Bridge House Pre-Prep School, London

The Farm

On the farm, there are goats and alpacas
Trees and apples
There are horses and donkeys
It is very cold in winter
But it is very cosy by the fire
There is no pollution on the farm
It makes me feel happy.

Michael Masterson (6)
North Bridge House Pre-Prep School, London

Save Nature!

We have to save the ocean,
To save the fish and coral,
To recycle plastic!
Protect the fish so they don't become extinct.
Help the creatures to survive.
Save the environment.
Save nature!

Xavier Mistry (6)
North Bridge House Pre-Prep School, London

My Future

The future sound tells me things.
The grass makes it fresh, trees make us glow.
It's time that we learn.
To help the future you need to put it right for us!
My future needs you.
Be you.

Daren Yi (6)
North Bridge House Pre-Prep School, London

I Love Polar Bears

I love polar bears
You are white and fluffy
Just like the snow you live in
You eat fish, I do too
You live in the Arctic
I hope it does not melt
I want to see you
I love you too.

Kailhan Varatharajan (5)
North Bridge House Pre-Prep School, London

The Penguin's Life

Penguins are black and white
And they live in Antarctica.
They only have three toes on their feet.
They waddle and wiggle and get in a pickle
If their belly goes faster than their feet.

Anaïs Strauss (6)
North Bridge House Pre-Prep School, London

A World Poem

W ander around the world.
O xygen comes from trees.
R emember the facts about the world.
L ions are actually cats!
D inosaurs roamed the world long ago.

Layla Zaghloul (6)
North Bridge House Pre-Prep School, London

Our Blue Planet

O cean, so beautiful!
C olourful fishes swimming around
E very wave is splashing
A nd lovely, green seaweed flapping
N ice bubbles popping everywhere!

Issy Armstrong (5)
North Bridge House Pre-Prep School, London

The Sea

I see umbrellas fluttering
I hear waves crashing
I go for a swim
I taste salty water
I see a crab dig
Mummy calls for me
It's time for ice cream
I feel happy.

Rocco Recksik (6)
North Bridge House Pre-Prep School, London

Our Planet

P retty big in my eye
L ook after it
A mazing place to live
N othing bigger in this world
E verything I need is here
T iny little house.

Matteo Naghib (7)
North Bridge House Pre-Prep School, London

Earth

Earth is the best planet because we live on it.
Astronauts explore the planets and they go back to Earth.
On Earth there are no moon rocks.
On the other planets there is no life.

Sashi Dimitrov (5)
North Bridge House Pre-Prep School, London

Our Planet

I like summer!
Summer is hot.
Summer is sunny,
The sky is blue.
Sun cream, hats, sunglasses,
Shorts and sandals.
The beach is exciting,
I play with the sand.

Georgina Taub (5)
North Bridge House Pre-Prep School, London

The Park

The park is cool and it is fun
When the wind blows the leaves fall
You can play on the slide
And you can play on the swing
There's a pond and all the ducks swim.

Xander Sijuwade (5)
North Bridge House Pre-Prep School, London

Volcanoes

Volcanoes
That are extinct
Don't have magma inside.
Volcanos have a liquid called
Lava. When it comes out, it dries
Up and turns into rock in time.

Timur Lim (6)
North Bridge House Pre-Prep School, London

Waste
A kennings poem

Whale killer
Fish trapper
Crab tangler
Fish squeezer
Toilet blocker
People killer
Bug killer
Farmer disaster,
Pollution helper.

Thomas Gatt (7)
North Bridge House Pre-Prep School, London

Ducks

D ucks like water
U seful feathers all around
C hatting sounds like quacks
K eep an eye on them
S ave the ducks!

Jack Lees (7)
North Bridge House Pre-Prep School, London

Pollution In Sea And Ocean

Fish live in the seas and oceans.
Fish need our help.
Save the fish.
Plastic kills the fish.
Stop throwing plastic in the seas and oceans.

Amro Elatfy (6)
North Bridge House Pre-Prep School, London

Be Friendly With Trees

To save our planet we have to protect nature.
We need to save trees.
Trees help Earth fight against pollution.
Be friendly with trees.

Gabriel Chazot (7)
North Bridge House Pre-Prep School, London

The Leaves

The leaves are green
The leaves are brown
They go and twirl
They never stop
They just twirl
More and more and more!

Sofia Smodis (6)
North Bridge House Pre-Prep School, London

Our Planet Earth's Ecosystem

Challenge facer,
Home of nature,
Blue and green ball,
This is where you are!

Fedor Kirichun (7)
North Bridge House Pre-Prep School, London

The Winter

Snow falls down.
Christmas is here.
Presents arrive.
Lots of cheer.

Leon Caville (6)
North Bridge House Pre-Prep School, London

Planet Plastic

The world was once a wonderful place,
It was fun, healthy, happy and had loads of space,
But in the 1980s a mysterious thing appeared,
It wasn't shiny, sharp, silly or cool, just as still as a tear,
More and more were made every day,
Being slaughtered or slain would make no difference today,
Our beautiful world was dark and grey,
Piles of plastic lay in dead hay,
Smoke and caps found under my pillow,
No more animals to brighten our willow,
Tears pour out of everyone's eyes,
No more fun, sun or jam on a bun,
It's the end of our planet,
What shall we do?
Start more factories, buildings and no more farms?
There is no more hope, just sleep it out,
Our world will always be like this without a doubt.

Harvey Lewis Thomas Lloyd (12)
Our Lady Queen Of Peace Catholic Engineering College, Skelmersdale

What Is Happening To The World?

Don't you feel at night suffocation in absence of light?
The future will be bright, only if the climate is right
Summers are getting hotter, faced with spells of drought
Our climate is now changing, it's true without doubt, animals are dying
Forest fires are burning, leaving a scorched and awful barren land
We think about our future and wonder what happens next
Maybe it's not too late or maybe it is, but let's show our respect and our regret and wonder what we can do with it
This is our world and what would we do without Earth?
Our disrespect for our environment will cost us dearly
The polar ice caps melt at a rapid rate
Polluting our natural environment

It's not something to celebrate
We must change fast.

Evie Scrafton (12)
Our Lady Queen Of Peace Catholic Engineering College,
Skelmersdale

The Ice Is Getting Thinner!

The ice is getting thinner,
It also starts to glimmer.
The bear, fluffy and white,
Can no longer put up a fight.
He's screaming for help in fear,
But no one can hear.
Starving, abandoned and floating away,
He has no family and no place to stay.
The ice is getting thinner, the bear starts to panic and cry,
He's thinking to himself nervously and asking, "Why?"
His breathing is getting faster while he's looking at the skies,
With all hope gone now, tears roll down his eyes.
The ice is getting thinner, the bear has now drowned,
The moment that it happened, he fell with a silent sound.

Kayden Lewin (11)
Our Lady Queen Of Peace Catholic Engineering College, Skelmersdale

The Young Palm Tree

Hey! I'm a palm tree!
I live on the sunny shores
Just above the ocean floors.
I've only been around a few months
But yet I'm getting smaller!
My fellow bird friends
Describe a shiny, strange tool
Chopping me up like a fish!

And not even a day later
I am nothing but a stump!
I can't grow anymore
And no birds can perch on my leaves
Or eat delicious coconuts
To gain needed protein.

And now I stand small and forgotten
Missing the carefree life I once had.

Kelsie Cook (11)
Our Lady Queen Of Peace Catholic Engineering College, Skelmersdale

The Wonderful World, Not So Wonderful

The trees are down,
The homes are gone,
The animals can't do anything,
We need to change.

Climate change,
The factories' gas,
It will destroy the world,
The ozone will crash.

The trees are falling,
The animals are roaring,
We need to change now,
Or this will be appalling.

If we don't change now,
We will have to pay,
Deforestation will get us back,
The world will fade away.

I hope this message affects us,
And we will change,
To save the day!

Lucas Ratcliffe (12)
Our Lady Queen Of Peace Catholic Engineering College, Skelmersdale

In The Forest

In the forest, in the forest,
Trees stand tall,
Every last one refusing to fall.

In the forest, in the forest,
The only sound around is the bird's loud call,
Animals all around, big and small.

In the forest, in the forest,
Trees no longer stand tall,
Every last one starting to fall.

In the forest, in the forest,
No more sound, not even the bird's loud call,
Animals hiding, big and small.

Peyton Kelly (11)
Our Lady Queen Of Peace Catholic Engineering College, Skelmersdale

Save Our Planet

Our planet is dying and we need to save it!
Trees are so special, they give us carbon dioxide, an essential to life
And they provide a cosy home for many adorable species
But we harmful humans are taking that away from them
How would you feel if a tall, scary giant chopped down your home?
How would you feel if you got killed to make someone a luxury fur coat?
Sometimes we take wildlife for granted and this needs to be stopped.

McKenzie-Leigh Gregson (12)
Our Lady Queen Of Peace Catholic Engineering College, Skelmersdale

The Pollution Disaster

The trees moving,
The rubbish in the sea,
Let the turtles be,
Scoop up the leftover disaster,
Don't let this be you.

As the morning rises,
The next day, full of surprises,
You must dispel the rubbish,
Scoop up the leftover disaster,
Don't let this be you.

As the sun sets,
The disaster's still around the turtle's neck,
Days pass by,
Save us from the disaster.

Macey-Leigh Levy (11)
Our Lady Queen Of Peace Catholic Engineering College, Skelmersdale

Saving Mother Earth!

This is our world
We are the world
This is our planet
Planet Earth
We and the animals
We share the joy Earth has to offer
We should treat it better
We should care more.

    E arth is our property
    A nimals need to be saved
    R educe, reuse, recycle
    T ogether we can
    H ealthy Earth, happy Earth.

Save the world
Save your future!

Lola McGann (12)
Our Lady Queen Of Peace Catholic Engineering College, Skelmersdale

Trees Falling Down

Falling, falling, it will start pouring.
Stop cutting down trees
And we might still have some leaves.
Please, please, we need these trees.
It's how we breathe, so leave the trees.
Look at the sea, it's going green,
Don't be mean.
Animals are dying and wildfires are rising.
Ukrainian children are crying,
Innocent people are dying,
The war is making children bored.

Olly McGovern (11)
Our Lady Queen Of Peace Catholic Engineering College, Skelmersdale

The Environment

The environment is slowly dying
And the green trees are getting filled with rubbish.
In Antarctica, the ice is melting and it can't be fixed.
The animals are terrified of drowning
And their environment is disappearing.
In the ocean, there's nothing but rubbish
And animals stuck in nets and rubbish.
This is unfair to the animals
Because they did nothing to us to deserve that.

Finley McLoughlin Cookson (11)
Our Lady Queen Of Peace Catholic Engineering College, Skelmersdale

Save The Trees

Destroying trees is mean, all because of greed.
Bees are great for trees and help with green.
Trees are set on fire all because of a lighter.
Bees should be let free and not held in captivity.
Trees are very green but getting set on fire as flames are getting higher.
Animals are losing homes all over different biomes.
Temperatures are getting taller but really they should be falling.

Raygn Lancaster-Lyness (12)
Our Lady Queen Of Peace Catholic Engineering College, Skelmersdale

Our Planet

Help protect the planet
Save the rainforest
Protect the Earth
Put an end to pollution
All the animals are dying off
Some are near extinction
And we aren't doing anything!
Once you cut a tree down
Grow another
Before you kill an animal
Make another
Before you throw away rubbish
Stop and recycle
Sleep, eat, recycle, repeat!

Jazmine Williams (11)
Our Lady Queen Of Peace Catholic Engineering College, Skelmersdale

Save The Environment

We need to clean our environment
People litter and throw everything in the sea
We need more bins so nothing gets wrecked
Animals are dying and need to be saved
The polar ice is melting
We need to stop pollution and act now
Together we can have a happy, healthy Earth
This is our world and this is our planet
So save the environment, save the Earth.

Hannah Moorcroft (11)
Our Lady Queen Of Peace Catholic Engineering College, Skelmersdale

The Environment

In a tree
Is a bee
That is free.

In the ocean
That has a motion
It has commotion.

In the ice
Isn't a prize
But it will freeze.

In the fire
That desires
Is a wire.

In an area
With pollution
It is not a solution.

In a forest
Is an honest bear.

Ketija Pajate (11)
Our Lady Queen Of Peace Catholic Engineering College, Skelmersdale

Pollution

P ollution needs to stop.
O ur world is slowly destroying our future.
L ittering needs to stop.
L ovely, peaceful world is waiting.
U s, the world is shared by us.
T ogether we can.
I n this, we are together.
O n this world, we work.
N ature rules this world.

Scarlett Macgregor (12)
Our Lady Queen Of Peace Catholic Engineering College, Skelmersdale

Our Planet

This is our planet
A planet we were made on
A planet we live on
A planet we should treat with respect
Trees grow
Waves crash
The sun shines
This planet needs saving
Plastic being picked
Trees being planted
No plastic in oceans
This is what we need
For our planet
Earth must be protected.

Kristers Kalnins (11)
Our Lady Queen Of Peace Catholic Engineering College, Skelmersdale

The Environment

In the ocean
That has motion
There is a lot of commotion.

In a tree
There is a bee
That is freer than ever.

In Australia
There is a fire
That will retire.

In the north
There is a wind
That has a mind.

In an area
With pollution
There is no solution.

Emilija Pajate (12)
Our Lady Queen Of Peace Catholic Engineering College, Skelmersdale

The Great, Green Forest

In the great, green forest there were a lot of good dreams,
All of the animals running and buzzing bees,
But then one night, when people wanted a fight,
They cut most of the trees and gave the animals a fright,
Taking all of the wood to make themselves look good,
And now people are dying whilst animals are dying.

Enzo Johnson (11)
Our Lady Queen Of Peace Catholic Engineering College, Skelmersdale

Planet Earth

P lease save me
L ive to save
A ct now
N o plan B
E arth is dying
T he animals are suffering.

E arth is our home
A nimals need to be saved
R educe, reuse, recycle
T ogether we can help
H appy planet, happy life.

Ethan Byrne (12)
Our Lady Queen Of Peace Catholic Engineering College, Skelmersdale

This Is Our World Now

This is our world
Planet Earth
Where things can talk
And play
But now it's
Not the same
Plastic has taken over
Please help us
Fight our fights
Help our Earth
Be precious
This is our planet
Planet Earth
We love it
But not as closely
As everyone else.

Tyler James (11)
Our Lady Queen Of Peace Catholic Engineering College, Skelmersdale

Save Earth

S top littering
A ctive protesting to save the world
V ariety of wonderful plants and animals
E arth needs our help.

E arth is dying
A nimals in danger
R ecycle plastic
T he atmosphere is burning the world
H ealthy ecosystem.

Matthew Hislop (12)
Our Lady Queen Of Peace Catholic Engineering College, Skelmersdale

Save Our Earth!

S top pollution.
A ct now.
V aluable planet of ours.
E arth is precious.

E arth is our priority.
A nimals need to be saved.
R educe, reuse, recycle.
T ogether we can.
H ealthy Earth, happy Earth.

Save our Earth!

Maisie Ridgway (11)
Our Lady Queen Of Peace Catholic Engineering College, Skelmersdale

Save Earth

S ave the planet.
A ct now.
V aluable planet of ours.
E arth is important.

E arth is our amazing planet.
A nimals want to be helped and fed.
R educe, reuse, recycle.
T ogether we can save our Earth.
H elp the planet.

Rebeca Palma (11)
Our Lady Queen Of Peace Catholic Engineering College, Skelmersdale

Nature

Words may rhyme here and there,
But climate change is everywhere.
There are trees and grass as far as the eye can see,
But they aren't as pretty as they were before, that I can guarantee.
Plants and nature are no longer pure green,
But this generation is obviously not too keen.

Juliana Varga (12)
Our Lady Queen Of Peace Catholic Engineering College, Skelmersdale

The Effects On Polar Bears

As global warming progresses,
The polar bears are left with hot messes,
With nothing left to do but melt with it.
One last piece of ice
That isn't there when it reaches night.
The sun shining
And the baby cubs whining,
This is why we need to save our planet.

Jorja Jones (11)
Our Lady Queen Of Peace Catholic Engineering College, Skelmersdale

Our World

Trees make the breeze,
Nature is crumbling,
The world's in your hands,
The fire is spreading,
The world's retiring,
We can fix this,
Just try and make an effort,
Help us,
We can do this,
Reduce, reuse, recycle,
Don't make promises.

Hope Sorrell (11)
Our Lady Queen Of Peace Catholic Engineering College, Skelmersdale

Save The Earth

S ave our Earth
A ct quickly
V alue our Earth and nature
E arth is our home.

E arth needs our help
A nd we need to help it
R euse to help
T ogether we can save our world
H elp our Earth.

Kaci Williams (12)
Our Lady Queen Of Peace Catholic Engineering College, Skelmersdale

Nature

The bees in the trees are in the hill,
If you look inside you'll see them thrive,
In an effort to survive.
The bees that help with pollination
Are suffering from deforestation.
The seas that are filled with pollution
Need to be solved with one solution.

Alex Rowles (12)
Our Lady Queen Of Peace Catholic Engineering College, Skelmersdale

Deforestation

D angerous
E ndangered species
F orest
O zone
R espond
E xtinction
S ituation
T errible
A crostic
T ension
I rresponsibility
O xygen
N ever before.

Oskar Slojewski (11)
Our Lady Queen Of Peace Catholic Engineering College, Skelmersdale

The Lost Frog

There was once a lost frog
And it got lost in the dark.
His name was Gerry
And he loved to eat flies
But he hated rotten pies.
Unfortunately
He had a lot of family
That always cried,
Sometimes they wore funny ties.
He was bad for his lies.

Poppy Causer (12)
Our Lady Queen Of Peace Catholic Engineering College, Skelmersdale

My Story In The Park

I was recycling
When I remembered my friend Michael,
I was surprised that I saw him in a disguise.
I went to get some ice cream
When my dog came running towards me.
The ocean has too much commotion
And lotion is too wet and slippery.
Save the Earth.

Summer Levy (11)
Our Lady Queen Of Peace Catholic Engineering College, Skelmersdale

Save The World

S top littering
A ct now
V andalism stops now
E arth is important.

E arth is amazing
A nimals need to be saved
R educe, realise, recycle
T ime to help
H elp and save Earth.

Damien Rakoncsa (12)
Our Lady Queen Of Peace Catholic Engineering College, Skelmersdale

Our Planet

O ur planet
U s, we and the animals share the Earth
R educe, reuse, recycle.

P rotect the Earth
L ove the Earth
A ct now
N ature
E arth is our priority
T ogether we can.

Carmel Pierce (12)
Our Lady Queen Of Peace Catholic Engineering College, Skelmersdale

Grass

Green, green grass
The world is gonna pass
Animals are dying
Whilst the French are frying
Greta Thunberg is crying
No more slimy snails
Birds are getting frail
The trees are getting chopped
Popcorn is popping.

Ellis Houghton (11)
Our Lady Queen Of Peace Catholic Engineering College, Skelmersdale

Look After Our Planet, No Matter What

This is our planet Earth
Reduce, reuse, recycle
Save all the animals and their homes
Together we can make a
Healthy Earth, happy Earth
Earth deserves better
Like a sit on the clear beach
Our Earth is valuable.

Kenzi O'Donnell (11)
Our Lady Queen Of Peace Catholic Engineering College, Skelmersdale

Help The Earth

E arth was once a wonderful place
A bright, clean, dazzling display
R ecycle and reuse every day
T he world is dying and we are the problem
H ow can we help? We can help by picking up litter.

Lacey Ledden (11)
Our Lady Queen Of Peace Catholic Engineering College, Skelmersdale

Ecosystem

- **E** nvironment
- **C** limate change
- **O** zone layer
- **S** ave our planet
- **Y** our future
- **S** olar panels
- **T** rees being planted
- **E** xtinct animals
- **M** ajor deforestation.

Isobel Farley (12)
Our Lady Queen Of Peace Catholic Engineering College, Skelmersdale

Purple

P urple is a beautiful colour.
U nder the light a wonderful colour.
R eading a book with purple drawings.
P ure colouring.
L oving this.
E levating in my mind, thinking of this.

Maddie Abbott (11)
Our Lady Queen Of Peace Catholic Engineering College, Skelmersdale

The Rainforest

T errorising the rainforest is not good.
R ats and other little creatures get their home destroyed.
E cofriendly is cool and it helps the environment.
E arth is running out of cold and fresh air.

Xavier Naumovicz (11)
Our Lady Queen Of Peace Catholic Engineering College, Skelmersdale

Our Planet

Big green environment,
Full of plastic pollution,
Save, save the Earth,
Protect before extinction,
Ruining this Earth with climate change,
Pollution and lots more,
We can help,
Dreams can come true.

Miley Rae Davies (12)
Our Lady Queen Of Peace Catholic Engineering College, Skelmersdale

Beauty Of Nature

Trees swaying side to side,
The waves crash and collide,
Sun rays shining down to the ground,
Volcanoes erupt, making a very loud sound,
Trees are being cut down,
And animal rights have still not been found.

Abiah Kamran (11)
Our Lady Queen Of Peace Catholic Engineering College, Skelmersdale

Environment

- **E** xtinct
- **N** ature
- **V** ulnerable
- **I** mpact
- **R** escue
- **O** ver
- **N** o more planet
- **M** ystery
- **E** arth
- **N** ot okay
- **T** errible pollution.

Jacek Kwapisiewicz (12)
Our Lady Queen Of Peace Catholic Engineering College, Skelmersdale

The Life Of A Tree

As a seed of a tree falls off
It goes to the ground
A few weeks go by
And the seed sprouts out of the soil
It feeds on water and solar light
It grows tall and wide
It cleans the world of pollution.

Leon Janowski (11)
Our Lady Queen Of Peace Catholic Engineering College, Skelmersdale

Our World

Our world was
A beautiful
Place. It had
The
Blue, blue
Sky,
Green, green
Grass,
But now it's
Black, black
Sky,
Dead, dead
Grass.
The world
Is ending.

Lee Ives (11)
Our Lady Queen Of Peace Catholic Engineering College, Skelmersdale

Nature

- **N** ever forget about this world
- **A** nimals dying
- **T** rees falling
- **U** nderstand our message
- **R** emember you can change this world
- **E** veryone has to work together.

Evie Hutton (11)
Our Lady Queen Of Peace Catholic Engineering College, Skelmersdale

A Burning World

Flames getting higher,
Koala bears running from fire.
The world is getting warmer,
Not everything has to be a diploma.
Trees are getting taken down,
But it is nothing like a scary hound.

Teegan Graves (12)
Our Lady Queen Of Peace Catholic Engineering College, Skelmersdale

The River

Tossing, turning
Rocks banging
Fish swimming
The river violently shaking
Water pouring
Rocks silent
Fish sleeping
River peacefully swaying
The moon shining brightly.

Amelia O'Brien Roberts (11)
Our Lady Queen Of Peace Catholic Engineering College, Skelmersdale

Environment

We need to help our Earth
Because of the lumberjacks chopping down trees
People polluting
We need to help the Earth by cleaning up
Putting our rubbish in the bin
To save our Earth.

Ayden Denton (11)
Our Lady Queen Of Peace Catholic Engineering College, Skelmersdale

Elephants

E lephants
L eave every
E lephant home so
P lease stop
H unting
A nimals and
N ot thinking of
T rees.

Daniel Spencer (11)
Our Lady Queen Of Peace Catholic Engineering College, Skelmersdale

Brass Monkey

Brass monkey, that funky monkey,
Brass funky monkey, that funky monkey,
Swinging through the trees
And swinging through the vines,
Brass monkey can very much fly.

Jake Chatterley (12)
Our Lady Queen Of Peace Catholic Engineering College, Skelmersdale

The Gladness Of Nature

Is this a time to be cloudy and sad,
When our Mother Nature laughs around;
When even the deep blue heavens look glad,
And gladness breathes from the blossoming ground?

Savannah Corrie (12)
Our Lady Queen Of Peace Catholic Engineering College, Skelmersdale

Stop The Fire

The trees and leaves feel like fire,
Their own environment is hanging on by a wire,
The scent of smoke steams in the air,
For all of our animals this is unfair.

Harley Goodier-Davies (11)
Our Lady Queen Of Peace Catholic Engineering College, Skelmersdale

Plastic

P ollution
L ife-threatening
A nimals
S aving our Earth
T rusting
I n fighting
C limate change.

Ava Smith (11)
Our Lady Queen Of Peace Catholic Engineering College, Skelmersdale

Environment

This is about making our environment safe
and clean
Making it less polluted
Don't make a mess
And if you do make a mess
Clean it up.

Zach Dickson (11)
Our Lady Queen Of Peace Catholic Engineering College, Skelmersdale

Protect The Forest

Fires growing higher,
Koala bears need to be freed from fire.
The forests are where animals can live,
But humans take away trees because of greed.

Isaac Moore (12)
Our Lady Queen Of Peace Catholic Engineering College, Skelmersdale

Back To Nature

I love to dwell in the forest wild,
Where giant pine trees pierce the sky;
A beauty spot where nature smiled,
A fitting place to live and die.

Bethany Brown (12)
Our Lady Queen Of Peace Catholic Engineering College, Skelmersdale

Take Care Of Earth

The world is a boss place
Planet Earth
This is our world
Planet Earth
We should look after it
Stop plastic waste.

James McCormick (12)
Our Lady Queen Of Peace Catholic Engineering College, Skelmersdale

Save Our Planet

Will you save the trees
And will you save the bees?
Keep the leaves green
And save the turtles, please.

Scott Pittman (12)
Our Lady Queen Of Peace Catholic Engineering College, Skelmersdale

Deforestation Danger
A haiku

In the nice forest
We promised and weren't honest
Deforestation.

Nathan Figura (11)
Our Lady Queen Of Peace Catholic Engineering College, Skelmersdale

Save The Animals

S ave the animals.
A nimals deserve a better life.
V olcanoes kill animals.
E very animal deserves a home.

T he world should be a better place for animals.
H aving a world without animals would be tragic.
E very animal is smart.

A nimals could make the world a better place.
N ever kill animals.
I think animals are cool.
M eaning we have to care for animals.
A nimals can be kind if you're kind.
L ook after animals.
S ave the animals from getting killed.

Graciella Kusi-Appiah (9)
St Paul's Catholic Primary School, Cheshunt

Save The Animals

A nimals are the most precious thing in the world.
N ever kill animals because they give you the world.
I t is important not to kill animals because they never do something wrong.
M any animals get injured or killed over the years.
A ny animal will not do anything to you. They are precious.
L ots of animals are killed. In one year, one million animals got killed.
S o we can protect animals, we can help them if we see one.

N o one should ever injure animals.
E very animal is special and they never hurt you.
E veryone and animals are precious and lovely, love them as you do.
D o animals injure? No. Do they kill you? No. So don't kill them.

H ave animals ever hurt you? No, of course not. Then why do you kill them?
E very animal is lovely and sweet, but killing is not.
L ovely animals get killed, but if we protect them they won't die.
P eople just kill animals for no reason, so now we will protect them forever and not kill them.

Ela Capar (9)
St Paul's Catholic Primary School, Cheshunt

How We Can Help The World

H elp the animals,
O ur planet needs our help,
W e need to help it.

W e need to work together,
E normous parts of our world are dying.

C old seas are filling up with litter,
A nd if we don't help, soon our world will die,
N othing will change unless we help.

H oneybees need us,
E co-clubs are good for the planet,
L ilypads are our frogs' homes,
P lease help the animals.

T all trees are dying,
H elp nature, it's done so much for us,
E verything is dying.

W ondrous animals are dying because of us,
O ur actions can change the world,
R hinos and turtles are losing their homes,
L ovely flowers are going brown,
D o not litter, you are killing our planet.

Yvette Van Molendorff (10)
St Paul's Catholic Primary School, Cheshunt

Stop Killing The Whales!

Stop killing the whales, they now have nothing to live for.
You're only killing them for food and meat.
Just let them be free and happy, not sad.
You're just wasting their energy, purpose and dreams of living.
They all probably had a goal for this year, to live and sleep.
Just let them sleep, dream, live, survive and love.
You're letting them down.
You're killing them for meat.
You cook then you eat them and kill their dreams.
You're killing them and you are so happy you killed them.
You're so happy that an animal has lost their life.

Oscar Overett (8)
St Paul's Catholic Primary School, Cheshunt

A Better Future For Our World!

This is how to help our planet,
Well, we shouldn't attack it.
Stop picking grass up from the floor,
Because it might even open doors.
You must always let the flowers grow,
If you don't, that's a no.
Stop cutting down our planet's trees,
If you don't listen, we will not breathe.
Reduce, reuse, recycle,
Don't drive, use your bicycle.
You should always, always pick up your litter,
So that your world won't be so bitter.
This is how to help our planet,
Now we know we shouldn't attack it!

Hannah Powell (10)
St Paul's Catholic Primary School, Cheshunt

Save The World

S ave the planet
A ll the trees are being cut down
V iolet flowers are dying out
E arth is heating up.

T rees are sad because they are getting cut
H ow did the world end up like this?
E verywhere is infested with pollution.

W orld is getting dry
O n the trees, birds and squirrels used to live
R ock and dry floor is what it is now
L ooking for food, the animals can't find any
D o stop, please.

Alessadro Moreno Mendez (10)
St Paul's Catholic Primary School, Cheshunt

The Enchanting Environment

E nchanting world
N ew planet for the people on Earth
V ideos about our world
I n this world people litter
R ecycle and reuse
O ur living creatures are found injured
N ever litter on this planet's ground
M ake a difference, a big one
E ncourage people to stop this irony
N obody should do this
T o make a difference, just please stop littering, animals are in poverty and some of us are affected by it too.

James Kelly (8)
St Paul's Catholic Primary School, Cheshunt

Camping

Camping...
The fresh, crisp air,
I can hear the river running everywhere.

Camping...
The crunchy, warm grass,
The sky like grey, unpolished brass.

Camping...
Early morning hot chocolate,
I've been here the longest.

Camping...
That swing by the river,
The cold water makes me shiver.

Camping...
My friend caught a crayfish,
S'mores are my favourite camping dish.

Camping.

Olivia Kelly (10)
St Paul's Catholic Primary School, Cheshunt

Our Planet

Forests are on fire, the situation is dire.
The grass should be fresher, not drier.
Litter is everywhere on the street,
Making the wildlife shriek.
I wonder if mountains will keep their peaks,
The pollution is making the air reek.
So, we need to do something, make a change,
The effect is like a mountain range.
We all need to form like a cave,
Because it's our planet that we need to save!

Lucas Layton (10)
St Paul's Catholic Primary School, Cheshunt

Save Our World!

Please remember, always recycle
And don't use a car, use your bicycle
It would be nice if we could have a normal, small world
Animals get trapped and they are so scared
Our planet is curled
So this is my word
This affects birds
Rubbish gets thrown in the sea
It's not good, so when will we not do this anymore?
If this stops, animals and people will live better lives!

Scarlett Curtin-McKen (9)
St Paul's Catholic Primary School, Cheshunt

Save The World

If you litter a lot, now's the time to stop
Animals are being injured by this
Save the turtles
Greens are turning brown
Gas is shortening oxygen
Flowers need greens you know
If we don't have greens, how will they survive?
It will be really dull.

Save the animals, please
Recycle, reuse
If we do these things
We can make the world a better place!

Poppy Ward (8)
St Paul's Catholic Primary School, Cheshunt

I Love Animals

I love animals
I think I always have
I love them like my siblings
And my mum and dad.

It upsets me when I hear
When they get hurt or die
Because God made us all
And it makes me want to cry.

I hope when I get older
And my children ask aloud
"Did you think about the animals?"
I'll say, "Yes," and that makes me proud.

Daniel O'Neill (9)
St Paul's Catholic Primary School, Cheshunt

Help The Environment

E arth needs help!
N ever give up
V icious animals becoming extinct
I mportant people are harming animals
R ecycle more!
O utstanding animals
N ationwide help
M eeting other people
E arth, amazing Earth
N ever hurt the world
T ogether we can be better.

We are better together!

Grace O'Sullivan (10)
St Paul's Catholic Primary School, Cheshunt

Beautiful Environment!

Help animals no matter what,
Care for your green space,
Whenever you are in it!
Help plants grow just like you,
And remember you should care for God's planet
Because everyone in this world is special.
We all know that you can help the world!
You can help by:
Picking up litter,
Being kind,
And most of all,
Making our world a better place!

Savina D'Oca (7)
St Paul's Catholic Primary School, Cheshunt

Our Planet

The forest and bees are being let down
It's concerning everyone in the town
So let us and the beekeepers do our part
And help save the lovely bees like a fruit tart
Also, save the forest, lumberjacks are killing them
It's like having bad phlegm
So maybe plant a tree and multiply if you're loving
Please help out and take a walk, the forest is giving.

Kieron Lusanta (11)
St Paul's Catholic Primary School, Cheshunt

Boy And A Plant

Somewhere, anywhere, as far as the imagination.
A boy met a plant, a plant met a boy.
He did not know it would bring the world joy,
A plant so green, so crisp and clean.
This is the one.
This may be a dream,
But it's up to you,
It could not just be a dream if you play your part,
The world could gleam,
It comes from the heart.
Save our world.

Kara Hodson (10)
St Paul's Catholic Primary School, Cheshunt

Animals, Amazing Animals

Animals are amazing
Animals are sweet
We need to keep them safe
And treat them well, please
The animals help us by giving us milk
So we need to help them by keeping them happy
The animals all keep us happy
So we need to keep them healthy
Without them, we wouldn't have food
So let's do them a favour
And not kill them from now on, please!

Liberty Connolly (8)
St Paul's Catholic Primary School, Cheshunt

The Clear Ocean

O cean, the clearest thing, you can see anything through it, you can see everything for miles.
C alm water waves sway up and down.
E veryone kept the ocean clean, there is not a single piece of rubbish seen here.
A nimals swimming around and jumping around.
N ight sky shining on the sea and it looks like the water is glowing around the sea.

Bianca Avram (9)
St Paul's Catholic Primary School, Cheshunt

Save Our Planet!

Save our planet!
Don't litter, recycle.
You don't know what our planet does for us.
So we should look after our planet!
Our planet looks after us so we should look after it!
Our planet gives us the ability to breathe and live.
By destroying our planet, we are destroying our home.
So don't throw trash on the floor, look after our planet.

Alexie Chitolie (9)
St Paul's Catholic Primary School, Cheshunt

Outstanding Earth

O utstanding Earth
U ngracefully people are destroying it
R emember to always recycle.

E veryone has to do what they can to save the Earth
A lways care for the Earth
R econsider your bad choices
T o have a better future, we all need to play our part
H ave a moment to think and be mindful!

Elisabeta Neculai (9)
St Paul's Catholic Primary School, Cheshunt

Our Planet

Lava, lava, lava, lava, lava.
Glistening and spurting out flaming lumps of rock and ash every second.
Exhaling ash and suffocating towns and cities lost to history.
Burning everything in view and puffing flames and smoke.
Beware its fiery wrath.
Then it cools and turns into rock with swirly patterns.
The leaping flames are a distant memory.

Aoife Esther Keady (10)
St Paul's Catholic Primary School, Cheshunt

Protect Animals

P rotect animals from disasters
R emember, animals are delicate and precious
O h, and give them food to survive
T ime to give animals their own time
E valuate and clean and scrub and wipe their shelters
C limate change means it's time to shelter our animals
T ime for animals to find freedom.

Olivier Kaszuba (8)
St Paul's Catholic Primary School, Cheshunt

Let's Make The Earth Great Again!

N ot everything is biodegradable.
A ct fast, let's change the world.
T he animals of our world are disappearing by the minute.
U nbelievably, climate change is melting the world.
R econsider your wrong choices and turn them right.
E veryone needs to do their part, let's save the planet!

Blake Smith (10)
St Paul's Catholic Primary School, Cheshunt

A Better Place To Live

My hopes and dreams are to make a better world to live in.
To make my dearest dream come true,
I'd love my gracious animals to live in fresh, green trees
That grow in this beautiful world that my people and I live in.
I wish I knew how to save the glorious world that I live in.
So please help me to save this lovely planet!

Maya Allen (9)
St Paul's Catholic Primary School, Cheshunt

Care For All Of The Animals

N o more throwing recycling on beaches or in the ocean.
A nimals need more love from humans.
T igers need to be treated all the same.
U nder the rocks, you will see tiny creatures.
R hinos need more air and to be looked after.
E lephants need extra care and plenty of food to survive.

Ellie-May Goldhawk (8)
St Paul's Catholic Primary School, Cheshunt

Nature Is...

Nature is full of wildlife roaming
And leaves blowing.
Nature is rivers moving side to side
And squirrels climbing trees.
Nature is birds humming
And woodland walks.
Nature is breathtaking images
And colourful animals.
Nature is plants rustling
And birds tweeting.
Nature is beautiful.

Jasper Palmer (10)
St Paul's Catholic Primary School, Cheshunt

What Am I?

I am hidden,
I am bumpy,
I am loud,
I am quiet,
What am I?

I am green,
I am blue,
I am grey,
I am yellow,
What am I?

I am creatures,
I am vines,
I am trees,
I am water,
What am I?

I am seas,
I am skies,
I am the Earth in danger.

Lorena Aliberti (10)
St Paul's Catholic Primary School, Cheshunt

God's Beautiful Creation

G od's creation,
O bey the commandments,
D o nice things in your life,
S ay God's words.

E veryone has a part to play,
A re you protecting the world?
R ally to save this world,
T he world is ours,
H ave a good, happy life.

Giovanni Arango Kasa (9)
St Paul's Catholic Primary School, Cheshunt

Animals Should Be Loved

A nimals are like humans.
N o animals should be treated wrong.
I love animals and you should too.
M y plan is to help animals be loved more.
A nimals fill our world.
L ook after animals, they all need your love.
S o we need to start caring more for animals.

Fearne Popely (8)
St Paul's Catholic Primary School, Cheshunt

Animals Are Everywhere

Animals living everywhere.
Monkeys swing to their homes.
Birds flying to their nests.
Animals are everywhere.
So don't cut down this home or they'll be sad,
And if you do, our planet will die.
So help the world, just by doing your part.
You can create a difference in the world.

Adriano Nicolaou (10)
St Paul's Catholic Primary School, Cheshunt

Nature

N ature is amazing
A nimals are in danger because nature is getting ruined
T oday you can help out by donating to your local charity
U gly weather is coming and homes are disintegrating
R eally bad amounts of animals are dying
E nhance nature's life.

Dexter Breaks
St Paul's Catholic Primary School, Cheshunt

Animals

A nimals are big and small.
N obody hurt the animals.
I am telling you not to hunt them.
M oney will help the monkeys survive.
A nyone, please help to take care of them.
L ook around and love the animals.
S ee them suffer and help them stay.

Fiana Miltiadou (8)
St Paul's Catholic Primary School, Cheshunt

Wildlife

Wildlife, you can imagine all the trees and plants swishing around the bay.
The big and small animals roaring through the green rainforest.
Think of the amazing wildlife with all those cute animals and the juicy fruit that sleeps on the rainy trees.
Now do not disrespect the beautiful wildlife.

Tommy Parry (8)
St Paul's Catholic Primary School, Cheshunt

Protect The Animals!

Animals need protection from hunters and poachers!
People are killing animals.
They have done nothing, so why kill them?
Animals are the most precious things in the world.
People are killing animals for their tusks and horns.
If people stop buying them, people will stop killing them.

Jude Smith (8)
St Paul's Catholic Primary School, Cheshunt

To Help Nature!

They sometimes say when it turns noon it is so black.
Nature keeps us alive, if it dies, so will we.
We need to take care of this world and the environment.
Stop using petrol cars that kill the world.
We need to help, so switch to an electric car to take care of the world.

Louie Costello (9)
St Paul's Catholic Primary School, Cheshunt

In The Summer

In the summer,
The sun shines brightly
Onto the warm grass of shimmering fields.
In the summer,
You can see joyful people smiling and laughing,
All in peace and harmony.
In the summer,
You see colourful flowers blossoming
And glimmering in the radiant sun.

Rees Ohene (11)
St Paul's Catholic Primary School, Cheshunt

Our Planet

Dazzling sunflowers wave in the tropical heat.
Wandering birds searching for meat.
The sunflowers are as bright as the heavens above.
The hummingbirds and bees suck up pollen and show their love.
The cloudless sky glows in the distance.
The rising sun is very consistent.

Luca Amodei (10)
St Paul's Catholic Primary School, Cheshunt

Our Beautiful Planet

O utstanding Earth
U should not litter
R ecycle your plastic.

E veryone, don't litter
A lways help our planet
R econsider what you're going to do
T ogether we can do it
H ave you started yet?

George Amdrose (9)
St Paul's Catholic Primary School, Cheshunt

Forest

F reedom for the animals.
O n the trees, the snakes slither around.
R unning and running, just like in the park.
E veryone sees the reindeer coming.
S ome animals are hunting each other.
T ry not to hurt them or hunt them down.

Reggie-James Miles (9)
St Paul's Catholic Primary School, Cheshunt

Leave Birds Alone

B irds are beautiful, leave them alone.
I t's hard to not hear them but leave their blasts of colour alone.
R ecycle to help these extravagant birds.
D on't hurt these creatures.
S lip these birds throughout the world.

Jacob Robins (9)
St Paul's Catholic Primary School, Cheshunt

Recycle

R ecycling is good.
E veryone should recycle.
C are about the world.
Y ou should put rubbish in the bin.
C are about these things.
L isten to the recycling signs.
E veryone should care about the world.

Christian Manaois (7)
St Paul's Catholic Primary School, Cheshunt

Amazing Nature

N ature is green and beautiful
A nimals are nature too
T rees, bushes and grass are nature
U nderground there is nature, like worms and more
'R ound the world there is nature
E very day you see it everywhere.

Alessia Caruso (8)
St Paul's Catholic Primary School, Cheshunt

Our Planet

I wasn't going to rhyme but I'll give it a try.
Do you really want nature to die?
For the trees to let out a sigh while being cut down
And for the animals to cry?
Or do you want mountains and water fountains?
Protect, don't pollute.

Ruby Doherty (10)
St Paul's Catholic Primary School, Cheshunt

Cars

Cars are not good for the environment, you know!
Please don't use cars, use bikes if you can.
When you're not using your car, turn it off.
Oxygen is important because we can breathe fresh air!
If you have an old car, please change it!

Meghna Boojhowon (8)
St Paul's Catholic Primary School, Cheshunt

I'm Just A Tree

Please stop!
I'm just a tree.
I try to last 333 years,
But I only last three...
We want you to stop,
No matter what!
Right now it's funny for you,
But in a couple of years,
It will be funny for me!
Hahaha!

Kameron Prodromou (9)
St Paul's Catholic Primary School, Cheshunt

The Blue Ocean

O ur oceans need our help to take the trash out of them.
C are about our oceans, please.
E xtinction is coming for sea creatures.
A ll of us can help the ocean.
N ever throw trash in the shiny blue ocean.

Maya Rosinska (8)
St Paul's Catholic Primary School, Cheshunt

Nature

- **N** ature is everywhere
- **A** nimals are endangered
- **T** ogether we can change the world
- **U** nbelievably, pollution is everywhere
- **R** ally up to get the Earth back in shape
- **E** ndangered Earth needs help.

Kayla Okeke (10)
St Paul's Catholic Primary School, Cheshunt

Nature

Animals are big and small.
Nobody hurt them.
We should look after nature because animals live there.
Keep nature clean for animals.
Littering is something that we shouldn't do.
Littering is bad for the environment.

Sidelya Kalen (8)
St Paul's Catholic Primary School, Cheshunt

Weather

Windmill turner
Icy blaster
Special guster in the sky
Sunny like the sun of mine.

Stormy nights of the kites
Rain flies like pies
Leaves fall like rules.

Weather is sweet
Oh, weather is clever.

Gabriel Hristov (8)
St Paul's Catholic Primary School, Cheshunt

Wacky Wildlife

To let things grow
You need to keep them in a sunny place
And water them and care for them.
Let the flowers grow,
Wildlife needs them, you know.
It is always good to go out to the park.
Wildlife is never bad for you.

John O'Sullivan (7)
St Paul's Catholic Primary School, Cheshunt

Forest

One day I walked through the forest
There were owls in the branches
There was litter so
I picked the rubbish up and put it in the bin
Then I picked up the rest on the floor
I saw some meerkats and I rubbed them gently.

Matteo Amodei (7)
St Paul's Catholic Primary School, Cheshunt

Nature

N ature is very fragile.
A nimals roam around in the woods.
T he cheetahs are agile.
U nited, we humans have to care.
R ecycling is good for plants.
E veryone, don't harm nature!

Carolina Platon (9)
St Paul's Catholic Primary School, Cheshunt

Litter In The Sea

We need to save the sea animals
They are in danger
Because people are putting bottles in the sea
And the sea animals are eating them
From now on we need to be kind to the sea animals
They are God's creations.

Kaiya Prodromou (8)
St Paul's Catholic Primary School, Cheshunt

Our Planet

In summer the trees blow in the breeze
And the sun sets at night,
You can chill with the sea,
It's a very good sight.
In summer you will find lovely lavender,
In the sun you will have lots of fun.

River Cullen (11)
St Paul's Catholic Primary School, Cheshunt

Our Beautiful World

N ever litter
A lways care for our world
T each others to care for animals
U nbelievably, the Earth is getting hotter
R ecycle your rubbish
E arth, amazing Earth.

Aiden Hussein (9)
St Paul's Catholic Primary School, Cheshunt

Our Planet

Let's think about trees
And how they are being chopped down
Let's think about the animals
Where are they going to live?
Let's come together
And bring this to an end.

Faolan Saunders (11)
St Paul's Catholic Primary School, Cheshunt

Our Planet

Muddy fields cover the countryside.
Trees hold their defence as strong winds push against them.
The sun hides as darkness pushes through.
Animals seek shelter as darkness covers the land.

Andy Cash (11)
St Paul's Catholic Primary School, Cheshunt

Save Our Planet

I am a sphere
I have people living on me
I hold so many countries
I have one moon
My colours are blue, green and white.
Who am I?

Answer: I am the Earth.

Ezekiel Baker (10)
St Paul's Catholic Primary School, Cheshunt

Our Planet

Lovely, colourful sunset painting the sky
Fresh, crisp air
Beautiful, long view running for miles
Trees dancing in the wind
Small birds singing to each other on the branches.

Malakai Amali Rowland (10)
St Paul's Catholic Primary School, Cheshunt

Our Planet

On our planet there are seasons which are:
Winter, which is the coldest season,
Autumn, not a cold or hot season,
Summer, the warmest season,
And spring, a rainy season.

Aurora D'Alessandro (10)
St Paul's Catholic Primary School, Cheshunt

Mother Nature

When you go to the forest or the park
You don't pick flowers off the ground
And please, please do not cut trees
I love trees, they give us oxygen.

Taylor Anthony-Alphonse (7)
St Paul's Catholic Primary School, Cheshunt

Our Planet

B eautiful sunsets
E asy to find cool shells
A mazing animals
C reatures all around
H elp our world.

Ella-Louise Whitmore (10)
St Paul's Catholic Primary School, Cheshunt

Litter In The Forest

You should pick up litter in the forest
Because wildlife really needs you to
Please help wildlife if you want the planet to stay healthy.

Mason Valladares (7)
St Paul's Catholic Primary School, Cheshunt

Help The World

I want to follow in Jesus' footsteps
And help the environment
And the animals
And the whole, entire world.

Gabriel Hristov (8)
St Paul's Catholic Primary School, Cheshunt

Love Jesus And Follow In His Footsteps!

I love praying every day.
I love following in Jesus' footsteps!
I love Jesus, he means everything to me.

Joseph Vieira Palushaj (8)
St Paul's Catholic Primary School, Cheshunt

Following In Jesus' Footsteps

Peace for everyone
Let the bees get honey from flowers
Be kind to everyone.

Hayden Paton (8)
St Paul's Catholic Primary School, Cheshunt

YOUNG WRITERS INFORMATION

We hope you have enjoyed reading this book – and that you will continue to in the coming years.

If you're the parent or family member of an enthusiastic poet or story writer, do visit our website **www.youngwriters.co.uk/subscribe** and sign up to receive news, competitions, writing challenges and tips, activities and much, much more! There's lots to keep budding writers motivated!

If you would like to order further copies of this book, or any of our other titles, then please give us a call or order via your online account.

Young Writers
Remus House
Coltsfoot Drive
Peterborough
PE2 9BF
(01733) 890066
info@youngwriters.co.uk

Join in the conversation!
Tips, news, giveaways and much more!

 YoungWritersUK 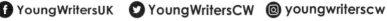 YoungWritersCW  youngwriterscw

Scan me to watch The Big Green video!